Space Voyager

Pluto and the Dwarf Planets

by Vanessa Black

Pluto

Bullfrog
Books

Ideas for Parents and Teachers

Bullfrog Books let children practice reading informational text at the earliest reading levels. Repetition, familiar words, and photo labels support early readers.

Before Reading

- Discuss the cover photo. What does it tell them?

- Look at the picture glossary together. Read and discuss the words.

Read the Book

- "Walk" through the book and look at the photos. Let the child ask questions. Point out the photo labels.

- Read the book to the child, or have him or her read independently.

After Reading

- Prompt the child to think more. Ask: What are your favorite facts about Pluto and the dwarf planets?

Bullfrog Books are published by Jump!
5357 Penn Avenue South
Minneapolis, MN 55419
www.jumplibrary.com

Library of Congress Cataloging-in-Publication Data

Names: Black, Vanessa, 1973– author.
Title: Pluto and the dwarf planets / by Vanessa Black.
Description: Minneapolis, MN : Jump!, Inc., [2018]
Series: Space voyager
Audience: Age 5–8. | Audience: K to Grade 3.
Includes index.
Identifiers: LCCN 2017035426 (print)
LCCN 2017029892 (ebook)
ISBN 9781624966897 (ebook)
ISBN 9781620318508 (hardcover : alk. paper)
ISBN 9781620318515 (pbk.)
Subjects: LCSH: Pluto (Dwarf planet) —Juvenile literature. | Classification: LCC QB701 (print)
LCC QB701 .B59 2018 (ebook) | DDC 523.49/2—dc23
LC record available at https://lccn.loc.gov/2017035426

Editor: Jenna Trnka
Book Designer: Molly Ballanger
Photo Researchers: Molly Ballanger & Jenna Trnka

Photo Credits: NASA images/Shutterstock, cover (left), 5; Walter Myers/Science Source, cover (right); KK Tan/Shutterstock, 1 (boy); Nostalgia for Infinity/Shutterstock, 1 (drawing); Popartic/Shutterstock, 3 (tablet); HIGH-G Productions/Stocktrek Images/SuperStock, 3 (planets); TRAIMAK/Shutterstock, 4 (girl); kalen/Shutterstock, 4 (tablet); JPL/NASA, 6–7, 8–9, 10, 11, 12–13, 14–15, 23tl, 23ml, 23bl,23br; wavebreakmedia/Shutterstock, 16–17 (boy); NASA, 16–17 (planet); John R. Foster/Science Source, 18; ESO/L. Science Source, 19; Alohaflaminggo/Shutterstock, 20–21; ixpert/Shutterstock, 23mr; AlexHliv/Shutterstock, 23tr; MarcelClemens/Shutterstock, 24.

Printed in the United States of America at Corporate Graphics in North Mankato, Minnesota.

Table of Contents

Small and Far Away

Pluto was once called a planet. Not now.

Today it is a dwarf planet.

Dwarf planets are small.
They orbit the sun.
Rocks orbit with them.

rocks

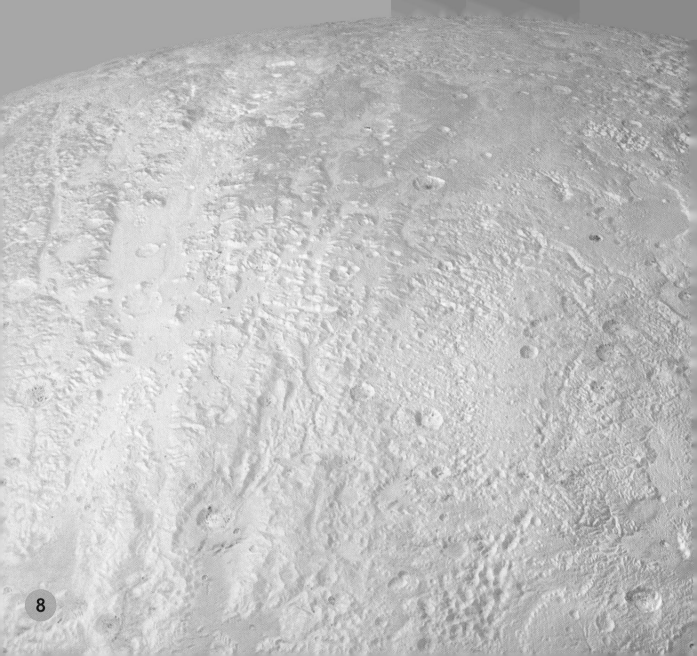

Dwarf planets are icy.
They are far from the sun.
It takes Pluto 248 years
to orbit the sun!

Pluto is red and gray.

Charon

It has a big moon.
It is Charon.

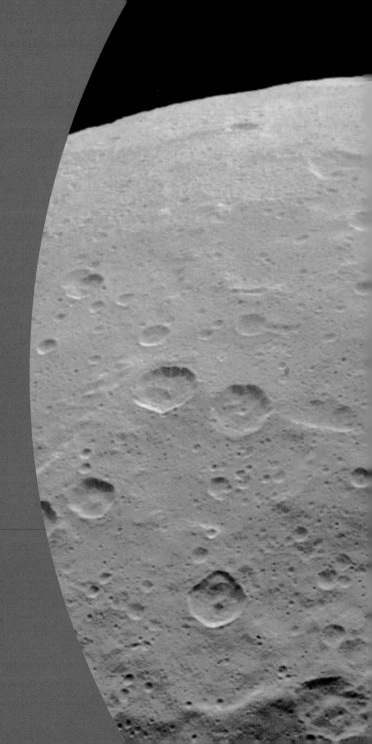

What are other dwarf planets?

Ceres is gray.

It has craters.

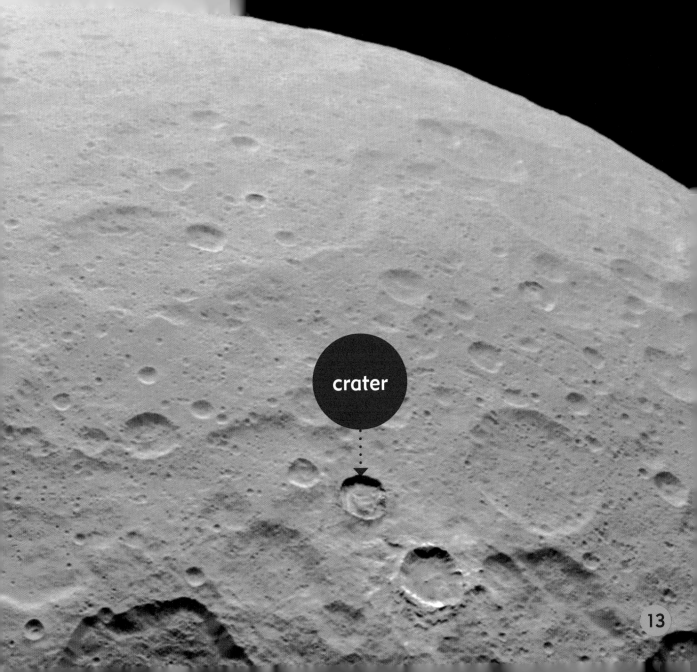

crater

How do we know?

We sent a spacecraft.

Haumea looks like an egg.

It has two moons.

Eris is the farthest away.
It has a tiny moon.

Eris

moon

It takes Eris 557 years to orbit the sun. Wow!

Space is big.
There could be more.
Maybe you will find one!

A Look at Pluto

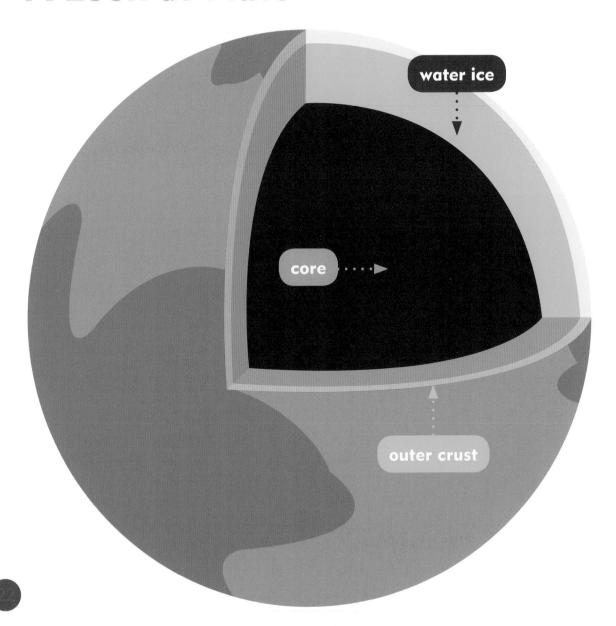

water ice

core

outer crust

Picture Glossary

craters
Large round holes.

orbits
Travels around in circles.

dwarf planet
A small planet that has other objects in its orbit.

planet
A large body that orbits the sun.

icy
Covered with ice or intensely cold.

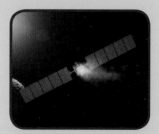

spacecraft
Vehicles that travel in space.

Index

To Learn More

Learning more is as easy as 1, 2, 3.

1) Go to www.factsurfer.com

2) Enter "Plutoandthedwarfplanets" into the search box.

3) Click the "Surf" button to see a list of websites.

With factsurfer.com, finding more information is just a click away.